MW01074402

Writings of John Woolman

Upper Room Spiritual Classics®

Selected, edited, and introduced by
KEITH BEASLEY-TOPLIFFE

UPPER
ROOM BOOKS®
NASHVILLE

WRITINGS OF JOHN WOOLMAN
Copyright © 2000 by Upper Room Books
Previously published as *Walking Humbly with God: Selected Writings of John Woolman*

Upper Room Books website: books.upperroom.org

Upper Room, Upper Room Books, and design logos are trademarks owned by The Upper Room, Nashville, Tennessee. All rights reserved.

Cover design: Tim Green | Faceout Studio
Interior design and typesetting: PerfecType, Nashville, TN

ISBN 978-0-8358-1650-2 (print) | ISBN 978-0-8358-1683-0 (mobi) | ISBN 978-0-8358-1684-7 (epub)

Library of Congress Cataloging-in-Publication Data

Woolman, John, 1720–1772.
    Walking humbly with God: selected writings of John Woolman / selected, edited, and introduced by Keith Beasley-Topliffe.
       p.   cm.—(Upper Room spiritual classics. Series 3)
    ISBN 0-8358-0900-5
    1. Woolman, John, 1720–1772. 2. Spiritual life—Society of Friends. I. Beasley-Topliffe, Keith. II. Title. III. Series.
BX7795.W7A3 2000   99-37742
289.6'092—dc21   CIP

Contents

Introduction

Many Christians feel drawn from time to time toward a particular social concern. Some may send money or sign a petition. A few will take further action—volunteering to help in a local project or contacting a legislator. And a very few will allow the concern to reorder their lives.

John Woolman was one of the very few. As a Quaker (a member of the Society of Friends), he was taught to pay particular attention to the interior movements of God's Spirit. A reluctance to write a bill of sale for a slave grew into a concern about slavery in general that sent him visiting other Quakers throughout the British colonies in America in the mid-1700s. He spoke at large Meetings and in private with individual slave owners, explaining why he believed slavery was wrong.

As Woolman's concern grew, it branched out into concerns for Native Americans, for Africans, and ultimately for all who were poor, oppressed, or exploited. In solidarity with the poor, he lived simply—even turning away customers when business demanded too much of his time.

Because he wanted his actions to be understood, he wrote a journal in which he explained the development of his special concerns and their effect on his way of life. He wrote pamphlets and essays that set out more systematic and objective views of slavery and other forms of economic exploitation. But the *Journal* stands as a spiritual classic, a look at the growth and development of a Christian soul seeking to know and do God's will in all things.

Woolman's World

The Society of Friends grew out of the experiences of George Fox, who was born in Fenny Drayton, England, in 1624. After years of seeking a deeper experience of God, he had a series of insights, or *openings*, in the late 1640s. He felt called to be a religious reformer, to rid the church of dependence on ancient symbols and external authority in favor of the direct experience of the Holy Spirit, the Inner Light. Worship in the societies he founded emphasized silent prayer until someone was prompted by the Spirit to share some word with the assembly.

Fox's attacks on traditional religion met with strong counterattacks, including prosecution for blasphemy. At one defense, he told the judge that he ought to tremble before God, leading the judge to call him a quaker. The nickname stuck and was eventually embraced.

In 1652, several similar groups joined with Fox in the Society of Friends. Many others were *convinced* (a term the Quakers preferred to *converted* or *convicted*). One of them was William

Penn, in 1667. Penn and others bought proprietary rights to the colonies of New Jersey and what became Pennsylvania. Many Quakers settled in these colonies, though when George Fox visited America in 1671–73, he found Quakers from New England to the Carolinas. Penn came to America in 1682 to help found Philadelphia.

The Society of Friends was organized in a structure of Meetings. The local society or perhaps a few banded together met monthly for business as a Monthly Meeting. This was related to a regional Quarterly Meeting and a much larger Yearly Meeting. Though local societies did not have pastors, gifted and Spirit-filled speakers could be given credentials as ministers with authority to visit other Meetings and even preach revivals. Woolman was such a minister.

Their religious convictions and experiences led Quakers to adopt a special vocabulary. Since the names of the days of the week and months of the year were often based on names of pagan gods, Quakers preferred to speak of First-day and Second-day, of First-month and Second-month, and so on. In addition to convincement (mentioned above), other special terms applied to the movements of the Spirit. Two are particularly important in reading Woolman. A moral objection or reservation about some action or possession was a *scruple*. The word could also be used as a verb, so that Woolman writes of scrupling to do such and such. The other term is *exercise*, which might refer to a strong pull to perform some action or to the inward struggle that came from resisting such a pull. Woolman compares some of his own exercises to the prophetic "burden of the Lord" often mentioned in the Old Testament prophets (translated as *oracle* in some modern translations) or to Jeremiah's description of God's message as "like a burning fire shut up in my bones."

Slavery, which was a fixture in all of the British colonies, took a variety of forms. Some slaves, both white and black, were set free after a fixed term of service. Others (almost exclusively black) were slaves for life. Many Quakers owned slaves, though as early as 1675 some had expressed misgivings about the practice. Still, there was an agreement to disagree peacefully. The few antislavery resolutions passed by Meetings in the early 1700s were advisory only, not binding.

Woolman's Life

John Woolman was born in Northampton (near what is now Rancocas), New Jersey, on October 19, 1720. He was the fourth of six children of Samuel and Elizabeth Woolman to survive infancy. At age twenty-one he moved to Mount Holly, about twenty miles east of Philadelphia, where he worked in a shop and later apprenticed himself to a tailor. By 1746 he was working on his own as a tailor and shopkeeper. Three years later he married Sarah Ellis. Their only surviving child, Mary, was born the next year.

In 1742, Woolman began to speak out in Meetings and was chosen as a minister of the Mount Holly Meeting. The next year he went on his first set of religious visits. As his concern about slavery grew, his visits became more extensive. In 1746, he spent three months visiting in Pennsylvania, Maryland, Virginia, and North Carolina. The next year he spent four months in Long Island and New England.

In 1754, Woolman organized his thoughts about slavery into a pamphlet: *Some Considerations on the Keeping of Negroes*. A much longer *Consideration on Keeping Negroes, Part Second* followed in 1762. He also began to write his *Journal*, edited from less formal records. In the meantime, he was largely responsible for convincing the Philadelphia Yearly Meeting to adopt a resolution (a "formal minute") urging Quakers to free their slaves and excluding those who bought or sold slaves from participating in Society business.

Woolman's visits continued. He made some of them on foot in order to better appreciate the condition of the poor. In 1761 he decided to give up dyed clothing, in part because he believed dyeing harmed the material (so that clothes wore out more quickly) and in part because he believed dye served mainly to hide dirt and so encouraged lack of cleanliness. In 1763 he visited Native American villages in north-central Pennsylvania. He began to write another pamphlet, *A Plea for the Poor*, though it was not published until after his death. Over the next few years he wrote several other pamphlets and essays and continued to prepare his *Journal* for publication.

In 1772, Woolman sought affirmation from his Monthly and Quarterly Meetings for a trip to the London Yearly Meeting in England. He left for England on May 1, traveling in steerage while other Quakers stayed in elegant staterooms. When he arrived in London on June 8, the London Yearly Meeting was in session. Woolman hurried over in his strange clothes, without taking time to wash, and was met with a less-than-enthusiastic welcome. A few Friends took the time to listen to him, and soon he was asked to address the whole Meeting. For the next several months he traveled to Meetings throughout England. In late September he contracted small-pox and died in York on October 7, 1772.

By 1784, Yearly Meetings in Virginia, Philadelphia, New York, and New England had all passed resolutions disowning members who still held slaves. In 1790, Quakers sent a memorandum to the first session of Congress urging the abolition of slavery throughout the United States.

Further Reading

Although Woolman had edited parts of his journal with an eye to publication, it was not published until two years after his death. An editorial committee made many changes, most fairly minor, but often complicating sentence structure. A later edition made substantial cuts. A reprint of this edition in 1871 with a new introduction by John Greenleaf Whittier became the basis for most later editions, including several now in print. In 1971, Oxford University Press published *The Journal and Major Essays of John Woolman*, edited by Phillips P. Moulton and based on the original manuscripts. It includes many helpful notes on Woolman's editing as well as a glossary and biographical sketches of people mentioned by Woolman.

For further information about Quakers, *The Faith and Practice of the Quakers* by Rufus M. Jones (Friends United Press) is the classic introduction. The journal of George Fox is available in various editions. Recent Quaker writers include Thomas Kelly (particularly *A Testament of Devotion*) and Douglas Steere, who wrote many books on the spiritual life including *Dimensions of Prayer* and *On Listening to Another.*

Woolman constantly quotes or alludes to the Bible. The only other book he mentions significantly is *Foxe's Book of Martyrs*. In 1567, John Foxe, an Oxford scholar, published this history of Christian witness from the first Christians through the early Reformation. His title was *History of the Acts and Monuments of the Church.* Later editions added further stories to bring the history forward another two and a half centuries and make Foxe a sort of brand name. It is readily available in a variety of editions.

Note on the Text

The underlying text for these selections is the Whittier edition of 1871, sometimes expanded in light of Moulton's edition of Woolman's manuscript. Selections have been edited for length and inclusive language. Punctuation, grammar, spelling, and in some cases, vocabulary, have been modernized. Woolman's sentences sometimes run on to great length with complex systems of subordinate clauses. These have been untangled and broken into shorter sentences. Direct quotes from scripture and some allusions have been conformed to the language of the New Revised Standard Version.

Childhood

From *Journal*, Chapter 1

Woolman began writing his Journal *when he was thirty-six, so the first three chapters are a spiritual autobiography rather than a day-to-day account. This selection about events of his childhood is the beginning of his story.*

I have often felt a motion of love to leave some hints in writing of my experience of the goodness of God. Now, in the thirty-sixth year of my age, I begin this work.

I was born in Northampton, in Burlington County, West Jersey, in the year 1720. Before I was seven years old I began to be acquainted with the operations of divine love. Through the care of my parents, I was taught to read nearly as soon as I was capable of it. I remember that as I went from school one day and my companions were playing by the way, I went forward out of sight. Sitting down, I read the twenty-second chapter of Revelation: "Then the angel showed me the river of the water of life, bright as crystal, flowing from the throne of God and of the Lamb." In reading it, my mind was drawn to seek after the pure habitation that I then believed God had prepared for his servants. The place where I sat and the sweetness that attended my mind remain fresh in my memory. This and similar gracious visitations had such an effect upon me that when boys used ill language, it troubled me. And through the continued mercies of God, I was preserved from that evil.

The pious instructions of my parents were often fresh in my mind and of use to me when I happened to be among wicked children. Having a large family of children, they would often, on First-days after Meeting, set us one after another to read the Holy Scriptures or some religious books. The rest would sit by without much conversation. I have since often thought it was a good practice. From what I had read and heard, I believed there had been, in past ages, people who walked in uprightness before God in a degree exceeding any that I knew or heard of now living. The apprehension of there being less steadiness and firmness among people in the present age often troubled me while I was a child.

I may here mention a remarkable circumstance that occurred in my childhood. On going to a neighbor's house, I saw on the way a robin sitting on her nest. As I came near she went off. But having young ones, she flew about and with many cries expressed her concern for them. I stood and threw stones at her. When one struck her, she fell down dead. At first I was pleased with the exploit, but after a few minutes was seized with horror at having, in a playful way, killed an innocent creature while she was caring for her young. I beheld her lying dead and thought those young ones, for which she was so full of care, must now perish for want of their mother to nourish them. After some painful considerations on the subject, I climbed up the tree, took all the young birds, and killed them. I supposed that better than to leave them to pine away and die miserably. In this case I believed that scriptural proverb was fulfilled, "the mercy of the wicked is cruel." I then went on my errand. For some hours I could think of little else but the cruelties I had committed and was greatly troubled. Thus the One whose tender mercies are over all his works has placed a principle in the human mind that incites us to practice goodness toward every living creature. If they only pay attention to this, people become tenderhearted and sympathizing. But when it is frequently and totally rejected, the mind becomes shut up in a contrary disposition.

About the twelfth year of my age, while father was out, my mother reproved me for some misconduct, to which I made an undutiful reply. The next First-day, as I was returning with my father from Meeting, he told me that he understood I had behaved amiss to my mother and advised me to be more careful in the future. I knew myself blamable and in shame and confusion remained silent. Being thus awakened to a sense of my wickedness, I felt remorse in my mind. On getting home I retired and prayed to the Lord to forgive me. I do not remember that I ever afterward spoke unhandsomely to either of my parents, however foolish I was in some other things.

Youthful Struggles

From *Journal*, Chapter 1

As Woolman continues to tell the story of his early years, he turns to the distractions of an active social life during his adolescence.

As I advanced in age, the number of my acquaintances increased. This made my way grow more difficult. Though I had found comfort in reading the Holy Scriptures and thinking on heavenly things, I was now estranged from them. I knew I was going from the flock of Christ and had no resolution to return. Hence serious reflections were uneasy to me, and youthful vanities and diversions were my greatest pleasure. In this road I found many like myself, and we associated in what is adverse to true friendship.

In this swift race it pleased God to visit me with sickness, so that I doubted of recovery. Then darkness, horror, and amazement seized me with full force, even when my pain and distress of body were very great. I thought it would have been better for me never to have had being than to see the day I now saw. I was filled with confusion. In great affliction, of both mind and body, I lay and bewailed myself. I did not have the confidence to lift up my cries to God, whom I had so offended. But in a deep sense of my great folly I was humbled before God. At length the word that is like a fire and a hammer broke and dissolved my rebellious heart. My cries were sent up in repentance. In the multitude of God's mercies I found inward relief and felt a firm assurance that if God were pleased to restore my health, I would walk humbly before God.

After my recovery, this awareness remained with me a considerable time. But by degrees I lost ground, giving way to youthful vanities and associating with wanton young people. The Lord had been very gracious and spoke peace to me in the time of my distress. I most ungratefully turned again to folly. At times I felt sharp reproof, but I did not get low enough to cry for help. I was not so daring as to do scandalous things. But my chief design was to excel in vanity and to promote mirth. Still I retained a love and esteem for pious people, and their company brought awe upon me. My dear parents several times admonished me in the fear of the Lord. Their admonition entered into my heart and had a good effect for a season. But since it did not get deep enough to lead me to pray rightly, the tempter found entrance when he came. Once I spent a part of a day in wantonness. When I went to bed at night, there lay in a window near my bed a Bible. I opened it and first cast my eye on the text, "Let us lie down in our shame, and let our dishonor cover us." This I knew to be my case and was somewhat affected meeting with so unexpected a reproof. I went to bed under remorse of conscience that I soon cast off again.

Thus time passed; my heart was refilled with mirth and wantonness. Pleasing scenes of vanity were presented to my imagination until I attained the age of eighteen years. Near that time I felt the judgments of God in my soul like a consuming fire. As I looked over my past life, the prospect was moving. I was often sad and longed to be delivered from those vanities. Then again my heart was strongly inclined to them. There was a sore conflict in me. At times I turned to folly, and then again sorrow and confusion took hold of me. In a while I resolved totally to leave off some of my vanities. But there was a secret reserve in my heart of the more refined part of them. I was not low enough to find true peace. Thus for some months I had great troubles. My will was unsubjected, and that rendered my labors fruitless. At length, through the merciful continuance of heavenly visitations, I was made to bow down in spirit before the Lord. One evening I had spent some time in reading a pious author. Walking out alone, I humbly prayed to the Lord for help that I might be delivered from all those vanities that so ensnared me. Since I was brought low, God helped me. As I learned to bear the cross, I felt refreshment come from God's presence. But I did not keep in the strength that gave victory, and so I lost ground again. The sense of this greatly affected me. I sought deserted and lonely places. There with tears I confessed my sins to God and humbly longed for God's help. And I may say with reverence that God was near to me in my troubles and, in those times of humiliation, opened my ear to discipline. I was led to look seriously at the means by which I was drawn from the pure truth. I learned that if I wanted to live such a life as the faithful servants of God lived, I must not go into company as before, according to my own will. But all the cravings of sense must be governed by a divine principle. In times of sorrow and abasement these instructions were sealed upon me. I felt the power of Christ prevail over selfish desires, so that I was preserved in a good degree of steadiness. Since I was young and believed at that time that a single life was best for me, I was strengthened to keep from such company as had often been a snare to me.

Learning to Listen

From *Journal*, Chapter 1

As a young adult, Woolman began to pay more attention to the movements of the Holy Spirit in his heart. Here he writes about learning how and when to speak at Meetings and about the beginning of his lifelong concern over slavery.

After a while my former acquaintances gave over expecting me as one of their company, and I began to be known to some whose conversation was helpful to me. Now I experienced the love of God through Jesus Christ redeeming me from many pollutions and helping me through a sea of conflicts, with which no person was fully acquainted. As my heart was often enlarged in this heavenly principle, I felt a tender compassion for the youths who remained entangled in snares like those that had entangled me. From one month to another this love and tenderness increased, and my mind was more strongly engaged for the good of my fellow creatures.

I went to Meetings in an awe-filled frame of mind and endeavored to be inwardly acquainted with the language of the True Shepherd. One day, being under a strong exercise of spirit, I stood up and said some words in a Meeting. But not keeping close to the divine opening, I said more than was required of me. Being soon aware of my error, I was afflicted in mind for some weeks without any light or comfort, even to the degree that I could take satisfaction in nothing. I remembered God and was troubled. And in the depth of my distress God had pity upon me and sent the Comforter. I then felt forgiveness for my offense. My mind became calm and quiet. I was truly thankful to my gracious Redeemer for his mercies. And after this I felt the spring of divine love opened and a concern to speak, and I said a few words in a Meeting in which I found peace. This I believe was about six weeks from the first time. As I was thus humbled and disciplined under the Cross, my understanding became more strengthened to distinguish the language of the pure Spirit, which inwardly moves upon the heart. I was taught to wait in silence sometimes many weeks together until I felt the rise that prepares the creature to stand like a trumpet through which the Lord speaks to his flock.

About the time called Christmas I observed many people, both in town and from the country, resorting to public houses and spending their time in drinking and vain sports, tending to corrupt one another; on which account I was greatly troubled. At one house in particular there was much disorder. I believed it was my duty to speak to the master of that house. I considered that I was young and that several elderly friends in town had opportunity to see these things. But though I would gladly have been excused, yet I could not feel my mind clear.

As I was reading what the Almighty said to Ezekiel respecting his duty as a watchman, the matter was set home more clearly. With prayers and tears I asked the Lord for assistance, and he, in loving-kindness, gave me a resigned heart. At a suitable opportunity I went to the public house. Seeing the man in a large group, I called him aside. In the fear and dread of the Almighty I expressed to him what rested on my mind. He took it kindly and afterward showed more regard to me than before. A few years later he died, middle-aged. I often thought that if I had neglected my duty in that case, it would have given me great trouble. I was humbly thankful to my gracious Father, who had supported me in this.

My employer had a Negro woman and sold her. He asked me to write a bill of sale while the man who bought her was waiting. The thing was sudden. Though I felt uneasy at the thoughts of writing an instrument of slavery for one of my fellow creatures, yet I remembered that I was hired by the year, that it was my master who directed me to do it, and that it was an elderly man, a member of our Society, who bought her. So through weakness I gave way and wrote it. But at the executing of it I was so afflicted in my mind that I said before my master and the Friend that I believed slaveholding to be a practice inconsistent with the Christian religion. This, in some degree, abated my uneasiness. Yet as often as I reflected seriously upon it, I thought I should have been clearer if I had desired to be excused from it, as a thing against my conscience. Some time after this a young man of our Society spoke to me to write an instrument of slavery, since he had lately taken a Negro into his house. I told him I was uneasy about writing it. Even though many of our Meeting and in other places kept slaves, I still believed the practice was not right. I asked to be excused from the writing. I spoke to him in goodwill. He told me that keeping slaves was not altogether agreeable to his mind, but that since the slave was a gift made to his wife, he had accepted her.

Growing Concern

From *Journal*, Chapter 3

By 1756 Woolman was in his midthirties, married with one daughter, and working as a tailor, shopkeeper, and farmer. He had already made several extensive trips throughout New Jersey and Pennsylvania and into other colonies, both north and south. His scruple against doing anything that might support slavery had grown into an exercise that demanded stronger action to oppose it. Here he talks about some ways he addressed the issue.

Scrupling to do writings relative to keeping slaves has been a means of various small trials to me. In these I have so evidently felt my own will set aside that I think it good to mention a few of them. Those who practice a trade and retailers of goods depend on their business for a living. They are naturally inclined to keep the goodwill of their customers. Nor is it a pleasant thing for young people to be under any necessity to question the judgment or honesty of elderly people—and more especially of such as have a fair reputation. Deep-rooted customs, though wrong, are not easily altered. But it is the duty of all to be firm in what they certainly know is right for them. A charitable, benevolent man, well acquainted with a Negro, may, I believe, under some circumstances, keep him in his family as a servant, on no other motives than the Negro's good. But we, as people, do not know what shall be after us. We have no assurance that our children will attain to that perfection in wisdom and goodness necessary rightly to exercise such power. So it is clear to me that I ought not to be the scribe where wills are drawn in which some children are made absolute masters over others during life.

About this time an ancient man of good esteem in the neighborhood came to my house to get his will written. He had young Negroes, and I asked him privately how he intended to dispose of them. He told me. I then said, "I cannot write your will without breaking my own peace," and respectfully gave him my reasons for it. He signified that he had preferred that I should have written it. But as I could not consistent with my conscience, he did not desire it. And so he got it written by some other person. A few years later, there being great alterations in his family, he came again to get me to write his will. His Negroes were still young. And since he first spoke to me, his son, to whom he intended to give them, was turned from a libertine to a sober young man. He supposed that I would have been free on that account to write it. We had much friendly talk on the subject and then deferred it. A few days later he came again and directed their freedom. I then wrote his will.

Near the time that the last-mentioned Friend first spoke to me, a neighbor received a bad bruise in his body and sent for me to bleed him. When I had done this, he desired me to write his will. I took notes. Among other things he told me to which of his children he gave his young Negro. I considered the pain and distress he was in and did not know how it would end. So I wrote his will except for the part concerning his slave. Carrying it to his bedside, I read it to him. I then told him in a friendly way that I could not write any instruments by which my fellow creatures were made slaves without bringing trouble on my own mind. I let him know that I charged nothing for what I had done and asked to be excused from doing the other part in the way he proposed. We then had a serious conference on the subject. At length, he agreed to set her free, and I finished his will.

Having felt drawn to visit Friends on Long Island, I set off twelfth of Fifth month, 1756, after obtaining a certificate from our Monthly Meeting. When I reached the island, I lodged the first night at the house of my dear friend Richard Hallett. The next day being the first of the week, I was at the Meeting in New Town. There we experienced the renewed manifestations of the love of Jesus Christ to the comfort of the honest-hearted. I went that night to Flushing, and the next day I and my beloved friend Matthew Franklin crossed the ferry at White Stone. We were at three Meetings on the mainland and then returned to the island, where I spent the remainder of the week in visiting Meetings. The Lord, I believe, has a people in those parts who are honestly inclined to serve him. But I fear many are too much clogged with the things of this life and do not come forward bearing the cross in such faithfulness as the Almighty calls for.

My mind was deeply engaged in this visit, both in public and in private. At several places where I was, on observing that they had slaves, I found myself under a necessity in a friendly way to labor with them on that subject. When a way opened, I expressed the inconsistency of that practice with the purity of the Christian religion and its ill effects manifested among us.

Thoughts on Business, Liquor, and Luxury

From *Journal*, Chapter 3

Here Woolman talks about the struggle between the demands of Christ and the demands of business. This leads him into consideration of strong drink and other luxuries.

Until this year, 1756, I continued to retail goods, besides following my trade as a tailor. About this time I grew uneasy on account of my business growing too cumbersome. I had begun with selling trimmings for garments. From there I proceeded to sell cloths and linens. At length, having gotten a considerable shop of goods, my trade increased every year. The way to large business appeared open, but I felt a stop in my mind.

Through the mercies of the Almighty, I had, to a good degree, learned to be content with a plain way of living. I had but a small family. On serious consideration, I believed truth did not require me to engage much in encumbering affairs. It had been my general practice to buy and sell things really useful. It was not easy to trade in things that served chiefly to please the vain mind in people. I seldom did it. And whenever I did, I found it weakened me as a Christian.

The increase of business became my burden. Though my natural inclination was toward merchandise, yet I believed truth required me to live more free from outward encumbrance. There was now a strife in my mind between the two. In this exercise my prayers were put up to the Lord, who graciously heard me and gave me a heart resigned to his holy will. Then I lessened my outward business. As I had opportunity, I told my customers of my intentions so that they might consider what shop to turn to. In a while I wholly laid down merchandise and followed my trade as a tailor by myself, having no apprentice. I also had a nursery of apple trees, in which I employed some of my time in hoeing, grafting, trimming, and inoculating. In merchandise it is the custom where I lived to sell chiefly on credit, and poor people often get in debt. When payment is expected and they do not have wherewithal to pay, their creditors often sue for it at law. Having frequently observed occurrences of this kind, I found it good for me to advise poor people to take such goods as were most useful and not costly.

In the time of trading I had an opportunity of seeing that the too liberal use of spirituous liquors and the custom of wearing too costly apparel led some people into great inconveniences. These two things appear to be often connected with each other. By not attending to the use of things that are consistent with universal righteousness, there is an increase of labor that extends beyond what our heavenly Father intends for us. And by great labor (and often by much sweating in the heat) there is a craving of liquors to revive the spirits even among such as are not drunkards. Partly by the luxurious drinking of some and partly by the drinking of others (led to it through immoderate labor), very great quantities of rum are every year expended in our colonies. We should have no need of the greater part if we steadily attended to pure wisdom.

When men take pleasure in feeling their minds elevated with strong drink and so indulge their appetite as to disorder their understandings, they neglect their duty as members of a family or civil society and cast off all regard to religion. Their case is much to be pitied. And where those whose lives are for the most part regular and whose examples have a strong influence on the minds of others adhere to some customs that powerfully draw them to the use of more strong liquor than pure wisdom allows, it hinders the spreading of the spirit of meekness and strengthens the hands of the more excessive drinkers. This is a case to be lamented.

Every degree of luxury has some connection with evil. If those who profess to be disciples of Christ and are looked upon as leaders of the people have the same mind in them that was also in Christ and so stand separate from every wrong way, it is a means of help to the weaker. As I have sometimes been greatly tired in the heat and have taken spirits to revive me, I have found by experience that in such circumstances the mind is not so calm or so fitly disposed for divine meditation as when all such extremes are avoided. I have felt an increasing care to attend to the Holy Spirit that sets right bounds to our desires and leads those who faithfully follow it to apply all the gifts of divine Providence to the purposes for which they were intended. If those who have the care of great estates attended with singleness of heart to this heavenly Instructor that so opens and enlarges the mind as to cause people to love their neighbors as themselves, they would have wisdom given them to manage their concerns without employing some people in providing luxuries of life or others in laboring too hard. But for want of steadily regarding this principle of divine love, a selfish spirit takes place in the minds of people, attended with darkness and manifold confusions in the world.

Receiving the Fruits of Slavery

From *Journal*, Chapter 4

In May 1757, Woolman and his brother Uriah set off on a journey through Maryland, Virginia, and North Carolina—1,150 miles in two months. In this selection from the beginning, just after entering Maryland, Woolman writes about his struggle over receiving hospitality from slaveholders.

Soon after I entered this province a deep and painful exercise came upon me. I often had some feeling of it, since my mind was drawn toward these parts. I had acquainted my brother with it before we agreed to join as companions. As the people in this and the southern provinces live to a great extent on the labor of slaves, many of whom are used harshly, my concern was that I might listen with singleness of heart to the voice of the True Shepherd and be so supported as to remain unmoved when face-to-face with people.

As it is common for Friends on such a visit to have entertainment free of cost, a difficulty arose in my mind with respect to saving my money by kindness received from what appeared to me to be the gain of oppression. Receiving a gift, considered as a gift, brings the receiver under obligations to the benefactor and has a natural tendency to draw the obliged into siding with the giver. To prevent difficulties of this kind and to preserve the minds of judges from any bias was that divine prohibition: "You shall take no bribe, for a bribe blinds the officials, and subverts the cause of those who are in the right."

Since the disciples were sent forth without any provision for their journey and our Lord said the workman is worthy of his meat, their labor in the gospel was considered a reward for their entertainment and therefore not received as a gift. Yet in regard to my present journey, I could not see my way clear in that respect. The difference appeared thus: the entertainment the disciples met with was from them whose hearts God had opened to receive them, from a love to them and the truth they published. But we, considered as members of the same religious society, look upon it as a piece of civility to receive each other in such visits. Such receptions are, at times, partly in regard to reputation and not from an inward unity of heart and spirit.

Conduct is more convincing than language. Where people manifest by their actions that the slave trade is not so disagreeable to their principles but that it may be encouraged, there is not a sound uniting with some Friends who visit them.

The prospect of so weighty a work and of being so distinguished from many whom I esteemed before myself brought me very low. Such were the conflicts of my soul that I closely sympathized with the prophet when he said in the time of his weakness: "If this is the way you are going to treat me, put me to death at once—if I have found favor in your sight." But I soon saw that this proceeded from the lack of a full resignation to God's will. Many afflictions attended me, and in great abasement, with many tears, my cries were to the Almighty for gracious and fatherly assistance. After a time of deep trial I was favored to understand the state mentioned by the psalmist more clearly than ever I had done before: "My soul within me is like a weaned child." Being thus helped to sink down into resignation, I felt a deliverance from the tempest in which I had been severely exercised. I went forward in calmness of mind, trusting that the Lord Jesus Christ, as I faithfully listened to him, would be a counselor to me in all difficulties. By his strength I should be enabled even to leave money with the members of the Society where I was entertained when I found that omitting it would obstruct that work to which I believed he had called me. As I copy this after my return, I may here add that often I did so under a sense of duty.

This is the way I did it. When I expected soon to leave a Friend's house where I had entertainment and believed that I should not keep clear from the gain of oppression without leaving money, I spoke to one of the heads of the family privately and asked him to accept pieces of silver and give them to such of the Negroes as he believed would make the best use of them. At other times I gave them to the Negroes myself, as the way looked clearest to me. Before I came out, I had provided a large number of small pieces for this purpose. Offering them to some who appeared to be wealthy people was a trial both to me and to them. But the fear of the Lord so covered me at times that my way was made easier than I expected. Few, if any, manifested any resentment at the offer. Most of them, after some conversation, accepted it.

Thoughts on Slavery

From *Journal*, Chapter 4

The description of Woolman's 1757 southern journey continues with his description of slavery and a Yearly Meeting in Virginia where Quakers debated how to address the issue of slavery.

From the time of my entering Maryland I have been under much sorrow. Lately it so increased upon me that my mind was almost overwhelmed, and I may say with the psalmist, "In my distress I called upon the LORD; to my God I cried for help." In infinite goodness, God looked upon my affliction and in my private retirement sent the Comforter for my relief. For this I humbly bless God's holy name.

The sense I had of the state of the churches brought a weight of distress upon me. The gold to me appeared dim, and the fine gold changed. Though this is the case too generally, yet the sense of it in these parts has in a particular manner borne heavy upon me. It appeared to me that through the prevailing of the spirit of this world, the minds of many were brought to an inward desolation. Instead of the spirit of meekness, gentleness, and heavenly wisdom that is the necessary companion of the true sheep of Christ, a spirit of fierceness and the love of dominion too generally prevailed. From small beginnings in error great buildings by degrees are raised. From one age to another these errors are more and more strengthened by the general concurrence of the people. As people obtain reputation by their profession of the truth, their virtues are mentioned as arguments in favor of general error. Those of less note, to justify themselves, say that such and such good people did the like. By what other steps could the people of Judah arise to the height in wickedness that gave just ground for the prophet Isaiah to declare in the name of the Lord, "No one brings suit justly, no one goes to law honestly," or for the Almighty to call upon the great city of Jerusalem just before the Babylonian Captivity, "See if you can find one person who acts justly and seeks truth—so that I may pardon Jerusalem"?

The prospect of a way being open to the same degeneracy in some parts of this newly settled land of America in respect to our conduct toward the Negroes has deeply bowed my mind in this journey. Though to relate briefly how these people are treated is no agreeable work, yet after often reading over the notes I made as I traveled, I find my mind engaged to preserve them. Many of the white people in those provinces take little or no care of Negro marriages. When Negroes marry after their own way, some make so little account of those marriages that with views of outward interest, they often part men from their wives by selling them far asunder. This is common when estates are sold by executors. Many whose labor is heavy are followed at their business in the field by a man with a whip, hired for that purpose. They are allowed in common little else but one peck of Indian corn and some salt, for one week, with a few potatoes. (The potatoes they commonly raise by their labor on the first day of the week.)

The correction ensuing on their disobedience to overseers or slothfulness in business is often very severe and sometimes desperate. Many times men and women have scarcely enough clothes to hide their nakedness, and boys and girls ten and twelve years old are often quite naked among their master's children. Some of our Society and some of the society called New Light Presbyterians endeavor to instruct those they have in reading. But commonly this is not only neglected but disapproved. These are the people by whose labor the other inhabitants are in a great measure supported—many of them in the luxuries of life. These are the people who have made no agreement to serve us and who have not forfeited their liberty that we know of. These are the souls for whom Christ died. For our conduct toward them we must answer before God who shows no partiality. Those who know the only true God and Jesus Christ whom God has sent and so are acquainted with the merciful, benevolent, gospel spirit will perceive that the indignation of God is kindled against oppression and cruelty.

In beholding the great distress of so numerous a people they will find cause for mourning.

From my lodgings I went to Burleigh Meeting, where I felt my mind drawn into a quiet, resigned state. After a long silence I felt an engagement to stand up, and through the powerful operation of divine love, we were favored with an edifying Meeting. The next Meeting we had was at Black Water and so on to the Yearly Meeting at the Western Branch.

When business began, some queries were produced by some of their members for consideration. If approved, they were to be answered hereafter by their respective Monthly Meetings. They were the Pennsylvania queries and had been examined by a committee of Virginia Yearly Meeting appointed the last year. They made some alterations in them, one of which was in favor of a custom that troubled me. The query was, "Are there any concerned in the importation of Negroes or in buying them after imported?" which was thus altered, "Are there any concerned in the importation of Negroes, or buying them to trade in?" And one query admitted with unanimity was, "Are any concerned in buying or vending goods unlawfully imported or prize goods?" I found my mind engaged to say that as we profess the truth and were there assembled to support the testimony of it, it was necessary for us to dwell deep and act in the wisdom that is pure. Otherwise we could not prosper. I then mentioned their alteration. Referring to the last-mentioned query, I added that since purchasing any merchandise taken by the sword was always allowed to be inconsistent with our principles and since Negroes were captives of war or taken by stealth, it was inconsistent with our testimony to buy them. Their being our fellow creatures and sold as slaves added greatly to the iniquity. Friends appeared attentive to what was said. Some expressed a care and concern about their Negroes. None made any objection in reply to what I said. But the query was admitted as they had altered it.

Since some of their members have heretofore traded in Negroes as in other merchandise, this query will be one step farther than they have hitherto gone. So I did not see it my duty to press for an alteration but felt easy to leave it all to God who alone is able to turn the hearts of the mighty and make way for the spreading of truth on the earth by means agreeable to God's infinite wisdom.

Tax Scruples

From *Journal*, Chapter 5

The French and Indian War (1754–63) brought new taxes to support the military action. How could Woolman, a servant of the Prince of Peace, pay a war tax? But how could he not pay when other Quakers had no problem with such taxes? Here he struggles with this new scruple.

A few years past, money was made available in our province for carrying on wars and to be repaid by taxes laid on the inhabitants. My mind was often affected with the thoughts of paying such taxes. I believe it right for me to preserve a memorandum concerning it. I was told that Friends in England frequently paid taxes when the money was applied to such purposes. I had conversation with several noted Friends on the subject who all favored the payment of such taxes. Some of them I preferred before myself, and this made me easier for a time. Yet there was in the depth of my mind a scruple that I never could get over. Sometimes I was greatly distressed on that account.

I believed that there were some upright-hearted men who paid such taxes, yet could not see that their example was a sufficient reason for me to do so. I believe that the spirit of truth required of me, as an individual, to suffer patiently the distress of goods rather than pay actively.

To refuse the active payment of a tax that our Society generally paid was exceedingly disagreeable. But to do a thing contrary to my conscience appeared yet more dreadful. When this exercise came upon me, I knew of no one under the same difficulty. In my distress I asked the Lord to enable me to give up all so that I might follow him wherever he was pleased to lead me.

Scrupling to pay a tax on account of the application has seldom been heard of before, even among people of integrity who have steadily borne their testimony against outward wars in their time. I may therefore note some things that have occurred to my mind as I have been inwardly exercised on that account. From the steady opposition that faithful Friends in early times made to wrong things that were then approved, they were hated and persecuted by people living in the spirit of this world. By suffering with firmness, they were made a blessing to the church, and the work prospered. It equally concerns people in every age to take heed to their own spirits. In comparing their situation with ours, it appears to me that there was less danger of their being infected with the spirit of this world through paying such taxes than is the case with us now. They had little or no share in civil government. Many of them declared that they were, through the power of God, separated from the spirit in which wars existed. Since they were afflicted by the rulers on account of their testimony, there was less likelihood of their uniting in spirit with them in things inconsistent with the purity of truth.

We, from the first settlement of this land, have known little or no troubles of that sort. The profession of our predecessors was for a time accounted reproachful. But at length their uprightness was understood by the rulers, and their innocent sufferings moved them. Our way of worship was tolerated, and many of our members in these colonies became active in civil government. Being thus tried with favor and prosperity, this world appeared inviting. Our minds have been turned to the improvement of our country, to merchandise and the sciences, among which are many things that are useful if followed in pure wisdom. But in our present condition I believe it will not be denied that a carnal mind is gaining upon us. Some of our members who are officers in civil government are called upon in their respective stations to assist in things relative to the wars. They are in doubt whether to act or to ask to be excused from their office. But if they see their brothers united in the payment of a tax to carry on the said wars, they may think their case not much different and so might quench the tender movements of the Holy Spirit in their minds. Thus, by small degrees, we might approach so near to fighting that the distinction would be little else than the name of a peaceable people.

It requires great self-denial and resignation of ourselves to God to attain that state in which we can freely cease from fighting when wrongfully invaded if, by our fighting, there were a probability of overcoming the invaders. Whoever rightly attains to it does in some degree feel that spirit in which our Redeemer gave his life for us. Through divine goodness many of our predecessors and many now living have learned this blessed lesson. But many others who have their religion chiefly by education and are not enough acquainted with the cross that crucifies to the world manifest a temper distinguishable from that of an entire trust in God.

Speaking Out

From *Journal*, Chapter 7

In 1760, Woolman went on a four-month trip to New England. In this selection Woolman speaks out publicly during a Yearly Meeting in Newport, Rhode Island, and privately to a group of slave owners.

And now an exercise revived in my mind in relation to lotteries, which were common in those parts. I had mentioned the subject in a former sitting of this Meeting. Then arguments were used in favor of Friends being held excused who were only concerned in such lotteries as were agreeable to law. Now it was opposed as before. But the hearts of some solid Friends appeared to be united to discourage the practice among their members. The matter was zealously handled by some on both sides. In this debate it appeared very clear to me that the spirit of lotteries was a spirit of selfishness and tended to confuse and darken the understanding. Pleading for it in our Meetings, set apart for the Lord's work, was not right. In the heat of zeal, I made reply to what an ancient Friend said. When I sat down, I saw that my words were not enough seasoned with charity.

After this I spoke no more on the subject. At length a minute was made, a copy of which was to be sent to their several Quarterly Meetings, inciting Friends to labor to discourage the practice among all professing with us.

Some time after this minute was made I remained uneasy with the manner of my speaking to the ancient Friend. I could not see my way clear to conceal my uneasiness, though I was concerned that I might say nothing to weaken the cause in which I had labored. After some close exercise and hearty repentance for not having attended closely to the safe guide, I stood up. Reciting the passage, I acquainted Friends that though I dared not go from what I had said as to the matter, yet I was uneasy with the manner of my speaking and believed milder language would have been better. As this was uttered in some degree of creaturely abasement after a warm debate, it appeared to have a good savor among us.

Though the Yearly Meeting was now over, there yet remained on my mind a secret though heavy exercise in regard to some leading active members about Newport who were in the practice of keeping slaves. This I mentioned to two ancient Friends who came out of the country and proposed to them to have some conversation with those members if a way opened. One of them and I consulted one of the most noted elders who had slaves. He, in a respectful manner, encouraged me to proceed to clear myself of what lay upon me. Near the beginning of the Yearly Meeting, I had a private conference with this elder and his wife concerning their slaves. Now the way seemed clear to me to consult with him about the manner of proceeding. I told him I was free to have a conference with them all together in a private house. Or if he thought they would take it unkindly to be asked to come together and to be spoken with in the hearing of one another, I was free to spend some time among them and to visit them all in their own houses. He expressed his liking to the first proposal, not doubting their willingness to come together. As I proposed a visit to only ministers, elders, and overseers, he named some others whom he desired also to be present. Since a caring messenger was needed to acquaint them in a proper manner, he offered to go to all their houses to open the matter to them. About the eighth hour the next morning we met in the meetinghouse chamber, the last-mentioned country Friend, my companion, and John Storer being with us. After a short time of retirement, I acquainted them with the steps I had taken in procuring that Meeting and opened the concern I was under. We then proceeded to a free conference upon the subject. My exercise was heavy, and I was deeply bowed in spirit before the Lord, who was pleased to favor with the seasoning virtue of truth. This created a tenderness among us, and the subject was mutually handled in a calm and peaceable spirit. At length, feeling my mind released from the burden that I had been under, I took my leave of them in a good degree of satisfaction. By the tenderness they manifested in regard to the practice and the concern several of them expressed in relation to the manner of disposing of their Negroes after their deaths, I believed that a good exercise was spreading among them. I am humbly thankful to God, who supported my mind and preserved me in a good degree of resignation through these trials.

Dyed Clothing

From *Journal*, Chapter 8

In 1761, Woolman continued to brood over the contrasts between rich and poor. He was determined to simplify his life in solidarity with the poor and to avoid all extravagances—things he saw as wasted labor. This led to a new scruple over the use of dyed clothing.

As I have thus considered these things, a question has arisen at times. Do I, in all my proceedings, keep to the use of things that are agreeable to universal righteousness? And then some degree of sadness has at times come over me because I accustomed myself to some things that have occasioned more labor than I believe divine wisdom intended for us.

From my early acquaintance with truth I have often felt an inward distress, occasioned by the striving of a spirit in me against the operation of the heavenly principle. In this state I have been affected with a sense of my own wretchedness. In a mourning condition I have felt earnest longings for the divine help that brings the soul into true liberty. Sometimes, as I have retired into private places, the spirit of supplication has been given me. Under a heavenly covering, I have asked my gracious

Father to give me a heart resigned in all things to the direction of divine wisdom. In uttering language like this, the thought of my wearing hats and garments dyed with a dye hurtful to them has made a lasting impression on me.

In visiting people of note in the Society who had slaves and laboring with them in brotherly love on that account, I have seen—and the sight has affected me—that a conformity to some customs distinguishable from pure wisdom has entangled many. The desire of gain to support these customs has greatly opposed the work of truth. Sometimes the prospect of the work before me has been such that, bowed down in spirit, I have been drawn into retired places and have besought the Lord with tears that he would take me wholly under his direction and show me the way in which I ought to walk. Then a strong conviction has revived that if I would be God's faithful servant, I must in all things attend to divine wisdom and be teachable. So I must cease from all customs contrary to this wisdom, however common among religious people.

As God is the perfection of power, of wisdom, and of goodness, so I believe God has provided that as much labor shall be necessary for our support in this world as would, if it were rightly divided, be a suitable employment of our time. We cannot go into extravagances or grasp after wealth in a way contrary to God's wisdom without having connection with some degree of oppression and with the spirit that leads to self-exaltation and strife. This spirit frequently brings calamities on countries by parties contending about their claims.

So I was fully convinced and felt an increasing desire to live in the spirit of peace. I have often been sorrowfully affected with thinking on the unquiet spirit in which wars are generally carried on and with the miseries of many of my fellow creatures engaged in them. Some are suddenly destroyed. Some are wounded and after much pain remain disabled. Some are deprived of all their outward substance and reduced to want. And some are carried into captivity. Thinking often on these things, using hats and garments dyed with a dye hurtful to them and wearing more clothes in summer than are useful grew more uneasy to me. I believe them to be customs that do not have their foundation in pure wisdom. The apprehension of being singular from my beloved friends was a constraint upon me, and so I continued in the use of some things contrary to my judgment.

On the thirty-first of Fifth-month, 1761, I was taken ill of a fever. After it had continued nearly a week I was in great bodily distress. One day there was a cry raised in me that I might understand the cause of my affliction and improve under it. Then my conformity to some customs that I believed were not right was brought to my remembrance. In the continuance of this exercise I felt all the powers in me yield themselves up into the hands of the One who gave me being. I was made thankful that God had taken hold of me by these chastisements, since I felt the necessity of further purifying. There was now no desire in me for health until the design of my correction was answered. So I lay abased and broken in spirit. As I felt a sinking down into a calm resignation, so I felt, as in an instant, an inward healing in my nature. From that time forward I grew better.

Though my mind was thus settled in relation to hurtful dyes, I felt at ease to wear my garments already made and continued to do so about nine months. Then I thought of getting a hat the natural color of the fur. But the apprehension of being looked upon as one affecting singularity felt uneasy to me. Here I had occasion to consider that things, though small in themselves, if they are clearly enjoined by divine authority become great things to us. I trusted that the Lord would support me in the trials that might attend singularity, so long as singularity was only for his sake. On this account I was under close exercise of mind in the time of our General Spring Meeting, 1762. I greatly desired to be rightly directed. When I was deeply bowed in spirit before the Lord, I was made willing to submit to what I apprehended was required of me. When I returned home, I got a hat of the natural color of the fur.

In attending Meetings this singularity was a trial to me— more especially at this time, since white hats were used by some who were fond of following the changeable modes of dress. When some Friends who did not know from what motives I wore it grew shy of me, I felt my way for a time shut up in the exercise of the ministry. In this condition, my mind was turned toward my heavenly Father with fervent cries that I might be preserved to walk before him in the meekness of wisdom. My heart was often tender in Meetings, and I felt an inward consolation that was very precious to me under these difficulties.

Visit to the Native Americans

From *Journal*, Chapter 8

In the summer of 1763, Woolman and Benjamin Parvin set out to visit Native Americans living in Wyalusing, Pennsylvania (about thirty-five miles northwest of present-day Scranton). The area was not yet settled by English colonists. The trip took about three weeks. This selection is from the outward trip, as Woolman considers how the natives were driven back from the coast into the wilderness.

My own will and desires were now very much broken, and my heart was with much earnestness turned to the Lord, to whom alone I looked for help in the dangers before me. I had a prospect of the English along the coast for upward of nine hundred miles where I have traveled. Their favorable situation and the difficulties attending the natives as well as the Negroes in many places were open before me. A weighty and heavenly care came over my mind. Love filled my heart toward all humankind. I felt a strong engagement that we might be obedient to the Lord while in tender mercy he is yet calling to us and that we might so attend to pure universal righteousness as to give no just cause of offense to the Gentiles—those who do not profess Christianity—whether they are the blacks from Africa or the native inhabitants of this continent.

Here I was led into a close and laborious inquiry whether I as an individual kept clear from all things that tended to stir up or were connected with wars either in this land or in Africa. My heart was deeply concerned that in the future I might in all things keep steadily to the pure truth and live and walk in the plainness and simplicity of a sincere follower of Christ. In this lonely journey I greatly mourned the spreading of a wrong spirit. I believed that the prosperous, convenient situation of the English would require a constant attention in us to divine love and wisdom, so they could be guided and supported in a way answerable to the will of that good, gracious, and almighty Being, who has an equal regard to all humankind. And here luxury and covetousness with the numerous oppressions and other evils attending them appeared very afflicting to me. I felt in what is immutable that the seeds of great calamity and desolation are sown and growing fast on this continent. I do not have words sufficient to set forth the longing I felt then that we who are placed along the coast and have tasted the love and goodness of God might arise in the strength thereof and like faithful messengers labor to check the growth of these seeds so that they may not ripen to the ruin of our posterity.

On reaching the Indian settlement at Wyoming, we were told that an Indian runner had been at that place a day or two before us and brought news of the Indians having taken an English fort westward and destroyed the people, and that they were endeavoring to take another. Another Indian runner came there about the middle of the previous night from a town about ten miles from Wyalusing and brought the news that some Indian warriors from distant parts came to that town with two English scalps and told the people that it was war with the English.

Our guides took us to the house of a very ancient man. Soon after we had put in our baggage there came a man from another Indian house some distance off. Perceiving there was a man near the door, I went out. The man had a tomahawk wrapped under his match coat out of sight. As I approached him he took it in his hand. I went forward, spoke to him in a friendly way, and perceived that he understood some English. My companion joined me, and we had some talk with him concerning the nature of our visit in these parts. He then went into the house with us and talked with our guides. He soon appeared friendly and sat down and smoked his pipe. Though taking his hatchet in his hand at the instant I drew near to him had a disagreeable appearance, I believe he had no other intent than to be in readiness in case any violence were offered to him.

On hearing the news brought by these Indian runners and being told by the Indians where we lodged that the Indians about Wyoming expected in a few days to move to some larger towns, I thought, to all outward appearance, it would be dangerous traveling at this time. After a hard day's journey I was brought into a painful exercise at night, in which I had to trace back and view the steps I had taken from my first moving in the visit. Though I had to mourn some weakness that at times had attended me, I could not find that I had ever given way to willful disobedience. Believing I had come thus far under a sense of duty, I was now earnest in spirit, beseeching the Lord to show me what I ought to do. In this great distress I grew jealous of myself, lest the desire of reputation as one firmly settled to persevere through dangers or the fear of disgrace from my returning without performing the visit might have some place in me. Full of these thoughts, I lay a great part of the night while my companion slept by me, until the Lord, my gracious Father, who saw the conflicts of my soul, was pleased to give quietness. Then I was again strengthened to commit my life and all things relating to it into God's heavenly hands and got a little sleep toward day.

Empathy

From *A Word of Remembrance and Caution to the Rich,*
Sections 4 and 6

*Sometime in late 1763 or early 1764, Woolman wrote a pamphlet
with the title, "A Plea for the Poor." He wrote it in his journal,
interrupting the journal entries for forty-six pages. While he was
in England, he reworked sections for several essays published there.
The whole was not published, however, until 1793, twenty-one
years after Woolman's death. The publisher gave it the title above.*

Our blessed Redeemer, in directing us how to conduct ourselves one toward another, appeals to our own feelings: "In
everything do to others as you would have them do to you."
Now, when some who have never experienced hard labor
themselves live in fullness on the labor of others, there is often
a danger of their not having a right feeling of the laborers' condition. So they are disqualified to judge candidly in their case,
since they do not know what they themselves would desire
were they to labor hard from one year to another to raise the
necessities of life and pay high rent besides. It is good for those
who live in fullness to cultivate tenderness of heart and to

make the most of every opportunity to be acquainted with the hardships and fatigues of those who labor for their living. So they will seriously ask themselves, *Am I influenced by true charity in fixing all my demands? Have I no desire to support myself in expensive customs because my acquaintances live in such customs?*

A wealthy man, on serious reflection, might find a witness in his own conscience that he indulges himself in some expensive customs that might be omitted consistently with the true design of living and that, were he to change places with those who occupy his estate, he would desire to be discontinued by them. Whoever is thus awakened will necessarily find the injunction binding: "Do to others as you would have them do to you." Divine love imposes no rigorous or unreasonable commands but graciously points out the spirit of brotherhood and the way to happiness, for which we must relinquish all that is selfish.

To pass through a series of hardships and to languish under oppression bring people to a certain knowledge of these things. To enforce the duty of tenderness to the poor, the inspired lawgiver referred the children of Israel to their own experience: "You know the heart of an alien, for you were aliens in the land of Egypt." Whoever has been a stranger among unkind people or under the government of those who were hard-hearted has experienced this feeling. But a person who has never felt the weight of misapplied power does not come to this knowledge except by an inward tenderness in which the heart is prepared to sympathize with others.

Let us reflect on the condition of a poor innocent man on whom the rich man lays heavy burdens, from a desire after wealth and luxuries. When this laborer looks over the cause of his heavy toil and considers that it is laid on him to support what has no foundation in pure wisdom, we may well suppose that an uneasiness arises in his mind toward one who might without any inconvenience deal more favorably with him. He considers that by his industry his fellow creature is benefited and sees that this wealthy man is not satisfied with being supported in a plain way, but to gratify a desire of conforming to wrong customs increases to an extreme the labors of those who occupy his estate. Then we may reasonably judge that he will think himself unkindly used. When he considers that the proceedings of the wealthy are agreeable to the customs of the times and sees no means of redress in this world, how will the sighing of this innocent person ascend to the throne of that great and good Being who created all and who has a constant care over his creatures! Those who toil year after year to furnish others with wealth and extravagances until they are wearied and oppressed by too much labor understand the meaning of that language, "You know the heart of an alien, for you were aliens in the land of Egypt."

Many at this day who do not know the heart of an alien indulge themselves in ways of life that occasion more labor than Infinite Goodness intends for people. And yet they feel compassion for the distresses of those who come directly under their observation. What if they were to change circumstances a while with their laborers and pass regularly through the means of knowing the heart of an alien and come to a feeling knowledge of the constraints and hardships that many poor innocent people pass through in obscure life? What if these who now fare sumptuously every day were to act the other part of the scene until seven times had passed over them and return again to their former states? I believe many of them would embrace a less expensive life and would lighten the heavy burdens of some who now labor out of their sight and pass through tight places with which they are but little acquainted. To see their fellow creatures under difficulties to which they are in no degree accessory tends to awaken tenderness in the minds of all reasonable people. But consider the condition of those who are depressed in answering our demands and labor for us out of our sight while we pass our time in fullness. Consider also that much less than we demand would supply us with things really useful. What heart will not relent? How can reasonable people refrain from easing the suffering of which they themselves are the cause, when they may do so without inconvenience?

The Tyranny of Self-Love

From *A Word of Remembrance and Caution to the Rich*,
Section 8

*This second selection from Woolman's pamphlet is sections 8 and 9
in the manuscript (of 15). The published edition combined the two
sections and renumbered the following sections. The idea of the self
as the worst tyrant of all binds together many of Woolman's regular themes: simplicity, pacifism, concern for the poor, and above
all, faithfulness to God in Christ.*

To labor to be established in divine love so that the mind is
disentangled from the power of darkness is the great business
of human life. Collecting riches, covering the body with finely
made, costly apparel, and having magnificent furniture operate
against universal love and tend to feed the self. So it is not a prop-
erty of the children of the light to desire these things. God, who
sent ravens to feed Elijah in the wilderness and increased the poor
woman's small remains of meal and oil, is now as attentive as ever
to the necessities of God's people. When God says to them, "You
are my sons and daughters," no greater happiness can be desired
by them. For they know how gracious a Father God is.

The greater part of the necessities of life are perishable so that each generation has occasion to labor for them. When we look toward a succeeding age with a mind influenced by universal love, instead of endeavoring to exempt some from those cares that necessarily relate to this life and to give them power to oppress others, we desire that they may all be the Lord's children and live in that humility and order becoming his family. Our hearts, being thus opened and enlarged, will feel content with a state of things as foreign to luxury and grandeur as the pattern our Redeemer laid down.

By desiring wealth for the power and distinction it gives and gathering it on this motive, people may become rich. But since their minds are drawn in a way distinguishable from the drawings of the Father, they cannot be united to the heavenly society where God is the strength of life. "It is easier," says our Savior, "for a camel to go through the eye of a needle than for someone who is rich to enter the kingdom of God." Here our Lord uses an instructive similitude. As a camel while in that form cannot pass through the eye of a needle, so someone who trusts in riches and holds them for the sake of the power and distinction attending them cannot in that spirit enter the kingdom. Now every part of a camel may be so reduced as to pass through a hole as small as the eye of a needle. Yet such is the bulk of the creature and the hardness of its bones and teeth that it could not be so reduced without much labor. People must cease from the spirit that craves riches and be brought into another disposition before they inherit the kingdom, as thoroughly as a camel must be changed from the form of a camel in passing through the eye of a needle.

When our Savior said to the rich youth, "Go, sell what you own, and give the money to the poor," though undoubtedly it was his duty to have done so, yet to enjoin the selling of all as a duty on every true Christian would be to limit the Holy One. Obedient children who are entrusted with great outward wealth wait for wisdom to dispose of it agreeably to God's will, in whom the orphan finds mercy. It may not be the duty of all to commit at once their substance to other hands but from time to time to look around among the numerous branches of the great family as the stewards of God, who provides for the widows and fatherless. But as disciples of Christ, although entrusted with many goods, they may not conform to sumptuous or luxurious living. For as he lived in perfect plainness and simplicity, the greatest in his family cannot by virtue of their station claim a right to live in worldly grandeur without contradicting him who said, "It is enough for the disciple to be like the teacher."

When our eyes are so single as to discern the selfish spirit clearly, we see that it is the greatest of all tyrants. Many thousand innocent people under some of the Roman emperors were confirmed in the truth of Christ's religion by the powerful effects of his Holy Spirit upon them. They scrupled to conform to heathen rites and were put to death by various kinds of cruel and lingering torments, as is largely set forth by Eusebius.

Now, if we single out Domitian, Nero, or any other of the persecuting emperors, that man, though terrible in his time, will appear as a tyrant of small consequence compared with this selfish spirit. Though his bounds were large, yet a great part of the world was out of his reach. Though he grievously afflicted the bodies of innocent people, yet the minds of many were divinely supported in their greatest agonies. Being faithful unto death, they were delivered from his tyranny. His reign, though cruel for a time, was soon over. And he in his greatest pomp appears to have been a slave to a selfish spirit.

Thus tyranny as applied to a man rises up and soon has an end. But consider the numerous oppressions in many states and the calamities occasioned by contending nations in various countries and ages of the world, and remember that selfishness has been the original cause of them all. Consider that those who are unredeemed from this selfish spirit not only afflict others but are afflicted themselves and have no real quietness in this life or in the future, but, according to the sayings of Christ, have their portion "where their worm never dies, and the fire is never quenched." Consider the havoc that is made in this age and how numbers of people are hurried on, striving to collect treasure to please minds that wander from perfect resignation. In the wisdom that is foolishness with God, they are perverting the true use of things, contending with one another to the point of bloodshed, and exerting their power to support ways of living foreign to the life of one wholly crucified to the world. Consider what great numbers of people are employed in preparing implements of war and the labor and toil of armies set apart for protecting their respective territories from invasion and the extensive miseries that attend their engagements. Meanwhile, those who till the land and are employed in other useful things in order to support not only themselves but those employed in military affairs and also those who own the soil have great hardships to encounter through too much labor. Others, in several kingdoms, are busied in fetching people to help to labor from distant parts of the world, to spend the remainder of their lives in the uncomfortable condition of slaves. Self is the bottom of these proceedings. Amid all this confusion and these scenes of sorrow and distress, can we remember that we are the disciples of the Prince of Peace and the example of humility and plainness that he set for us without feeling an earnest desire to be disentangled from everything connected with selfish customs in food, in clothing, in houses, and in all other things? We are of Christ's family. By walking as he walked, we may stand in that uprightness in which we were first made and have no fellowship with those inventions that people in their fallen wisdom have sought out.

Identification with the Poor

From *Journal*, Chapter 12

In 1772, Woolman went to England to share his concerns about slavery and the poor with Meetings there. Much of this selection, however, deals with a vision Woolman had while sick with pleurisy in January of 1770. This is one of Woolman's last journal entries. He died a month and a half later.

Twenty-third of Eighth-month.—I was this day at Preston Patrick, and had a comfortable Meeting. I have several times been entertained at the houses of Friends who had various things about them that had the appearance of outward greatness. As I have kept inward, way has opened for conversation with such in private in which divine goodness has favored us together with heart-tendering times.

Twenty-sixth of Eighth-month.—Being now at George Crosfield's, in the county of Westmoreland, I feel a concern to commit to writing the following uncommon circumstance.

In a time of sickness with the pleurisy a little more than two years and a half ago, I was brought so near the gates of death that I forgot my name. Being then desirous to know who I was, I saw a mass of matter of a dull, gloomy color between the south and the east. I was informed that this mass was human beings in as great misery as they could be and live. I was mixed with them and henceforth might not consider myself as a distinct or separate being. I remained in this state several hours. I then heard a soft, melodious voice, more pure and harmonious than any I had heard with my ears before. I believed it was the voice of an angel who spoke to the other angels. The words were, "John Woolman is dead." I soon remembered that I was once John Woolman. Since I was sure that I was alive in the body, I greatly wondered what that heavenly voice could mean. I believed beyond doubting that it was the voice of a holy angel. But as yet it was a mystery to me.

I was then carried in spirit to the mines where poor oppressed people were digging rich treasures for those called Christians and heard them blaspheme the name of Christ. I was grieved at this, for his name was precious to me. I was then informed that these heathens were told that those who oppressed them were the followers of Christ, and they said among themselves, "If Christ directed them to use us in this way, then Christ is a cruel tyrant."

All this time the song of the angel remained a mystery. In the morning, when my dear wife and some others came to my bedside, I asked them if they knew who I was. They told me I was John Woolman and thought I was light-headed, for I did not tell them what the angel said. I was not disposed to talk much to anyone, but was very desirous to get so deep that I might understand this mystery.

My tongue was often so dry that I could not speak till I had moved it about and gathered some moisture. As I lay still for a time, I at length felt a divine power prepare my mouth to speak. Then I said, "I have been crucified with Christ; and it is no longer I who live, but it is Christ who lives in me. And the life I now live in the flesh I live by faith in the Son of God, who loved me and gave himself for me." Then the mystery was opened and I perceived there was joy in heaven over a sinner who had repented. The words *John Woolman is dead* meant no more than the death of my own will.

My natural understanding now returned as before. I saw that people setting off their tables with silver vessels when entertaining were often stained with worldly glory and that in the present state of things I should take heed how I fed myself out of such vessels. Going to our Monthly Meeting soon after my recovery, I dined at a Friend's house where drink was brought in silver vessels and not in any other. Since I wanted something to drink, I told him my case with weeping. He ordered some drink for me in another vessel. I afterward went through the same exercise in several Friends' houses in America, as well as in England. I have cause to acknowledge with humble reverence the loving-kindness of my heavenly Father, who has preserved me in such a tender frame of mind that none, I believe, has ever been offended at what I have said on that subject.

After this sickness I did not speak in public Meetings for worship for nearly one year. But my mind was very often in company with the oppressed slaves as I sat in Meetings. Though under God's dispensation I was shut up from speaking, yet the spring of the gospel ministry was many times lovingly opened in me. The divine gift operated by abundance of weeping in feeling the oppression of this people. Although it is so long since I passed through this dispensation, the matter remains fresh and lively in my mind, and I believe it safest for me to commit it to writing.

Appendix

Reading Spiritual Classics for Personal and Group Formation

M any Christians today are searching for more spiritual depth, for something more than simply being good church members. That quest may send them to the spiritual practices of New Age movements or of Eastern religions such as Zen Buddhism. Christians, though, have their own long spiritual tradition, a tradition rich with wisdom, variety, and depth.

The great spiritual classics testify to that depth. They do not concern themselves with mystical flights for a spiritual elite. Rather, they contain very practical advice and insights that can support and shape the spiritual growth of any Christian. We can all benefit by sitting at the feet of the masters (both male and female) of Christian spirituality.

Reading spiritual classics is different from most of the reading we do. We have learned to read to master a text and extract information from it. We tend to read quickly, to get through a text. And we summarize as we read, seeking the main point. In reading spiritual classics, though, we allow the text to master and form us. Such formative reading goes more slowly, more reflectively, allowing time for God to speak to us through the text. God's word for us may come as easily from a minor point or even an aside as from the major point.

Formative reading requires that you approach the text in humility. Read as a seeker, not an expert. Don't demand that the text meet your expectations for what an "enlightened" author should write. Humility means accepting the author as another imperfect human, a product of his or her own time and situation. Learn to celebrate what is foundational in an author's writing without being overly disturbed by what is peculiar to the author's life and times. Trust the text as a gift from both God and the author, offered to you for your benefit—to help you grow in Christ.

To read formatively, you must also slow down. Feel free to reread a passage that seems to speak specially to you. Stop from time to time to reflect on what you have been reading. Keep a journal for these reflections. Often the act of writing can itself prompt further, deeper reflection. Keep your notebook open and your pencil in hand as you read. You might not get back to that wonderful insight later. Don't worry that you are not getting through an entire passage—or even the first paragraph! Formative reading is about depth rather than breadth, quality rather than quantity. As you read, seek God's direction for your own life. Timeless truths have their place but may not be what is most important for your own formation here and now.

As you read the passage, you might keep some of these questions running through your mind:

- How is what I'm reading true of my own life? Where does it reflect my own *experience*?
- How does this text challenge me? What new *direction* does it offer me?
- What must I change to put what I am reading into practice? How can I *incarnate* it, let this word become flesh in my life?

You might also devote special attention to sections that upset you. What is the source of the disturbance? Do you want to argue theology? Are you turned off by cultural differences? Or have you been skewered by an insight that would turn your life upside down if you took it seriously? Let your journal be a dialogue with the text.

If you find yourself moving from reading the text to chewing over its implications to praying, that's great! Spiritual reading is really the first step in an ancient way of prayer called *lectio divina* or "divine reading." Reading leads naturally into reflection on what you have read (meditation). As you reflect on what the text might mean for your life, you may well want to ask for God's help in living out any new insights or direction you have perceived (prayer). Sometimes such prayer may lead you further into silently abiding in God's presence (contemplation). And, of course, the process is only really completed when it begins to make a difference in the way we live (incarnation).

As good as it is to read spiritual classics in solitude, it is even better to join with others in a small group for mutual formation or "spiritual direction in common." This is *not* the same as a study group that talks about spiritual classics. A group for mutual formation would have similar goals as for an individual's reading: to allow the text to shine its light on the *experiences* of the group members, to suggest new *directions* for their lives and practical ways of *incarnating* these directions. Such a group might agree to focus on one short passage from a classic at each Meeting (even if members have read more). Discussion usually goes much deeper if all the members have already read and reflected on the passage before the Meeting and bring their journals.

Such groups need to watch for several potential problems. It is easy to go off on a tangent (especially if it takes the focus off the members' own experience and onto generalities). At such times a group leader might bring the group's attention back to the text: "What does our author say about that?" Or, "How do we experience that in our own lives?" When a group member shares a problem, others may be tempted to try to "fix" it. This is much less helpful than sharing similar experiences and how they were handled (for good or ill). "Sharing" someone else's problems (whether that person is in or out of the group) should be strongly discouraged.

One person could be designated as leader, to be responsible for opening and closing prayers; to be the first to share or respond to the text; and to keep notes during the discussion to highlight recurring themes, challenges, directives, or practical steps. These responsibilities could also be shared among several members of the group or rotated.

For further information about formative reading of spiritual classics, try *A Practical Guide to Spiritual Reading* by Susan Annette Muto. *Shaped by the Word: The Power of Scripture in Spiritual Formation* by M. Robert Mulholland Jr. covers formative reading of the Bible. *Good Things Happen: Experiencing Community in Small Groups* by Dick Westley is an excellent resource on forming small groups of all kinds.